DRAWING, PAINTING and PRINTING

Ideas and illustrations by

GIL JOHANSEN

Contents:

Published in Great Britain by World Distributors (Manchester) Limited,
P.O. Box 111, 12 Lever Street, Manchester M60 1TS

PRINTED IN ITALY

SBN 7235 0554 3

PENCIL SKETCHING

There are many ways in which a sketch can be shaded. You can, of course, use pencils with leads of different hardness or vary your pressure on the paper. But there is also another possibility; that is to use patterns or hatching and crosshatching. You can contrast different facets of an object against each other by covering one part with dots, another with slanting lines and another with squares. In this way you can give a drawing life and the picture becomes more interesting than if you only shade it in the ordinary way.

In the picture of a palette on the next page is shown an example of the different possibilities but you will be sure to think of many more for yourself. The old man up on the left on the next page is "coloured" by the clever use of a pencil. I am sure you will think the effect is very good.

This technique is particularly suitable for distinguishing between different articles of clothing.

Here you can exploit pattern or hatching technique.

OUTLINES OR "HELP" LINES

It doesn't matter wheth-
er you want to draw a
big house or a tiny beetle,
in both cases if you want

to get a good result, you
must first outline the motif. Begin the drawing
with thin, light
strokes and conti-

nue to sketch until you have got some similarity to the object you are drawing.

When you think you have achieved a good likeness, draw in definite contours with strong strokes. Lastly, finish off the sketch and rub out the "help" lines.

POTATO PRINTS

Potato printing is a simple but very interesting method of printing, which anyone can learn and get much pleasure from. On the next two pages are shown examples of different effects you can achieve with the help of some raw potatoes, a sharp knife and water colours. You can print on almost any material which has a smooth surface and which will not spoil the colours. Paper and closely woven fabric are ideal. The paint can be either water colours or poster paints.

The cleaned potatoes should be cut with a sharp knife so as to get an even surface on which

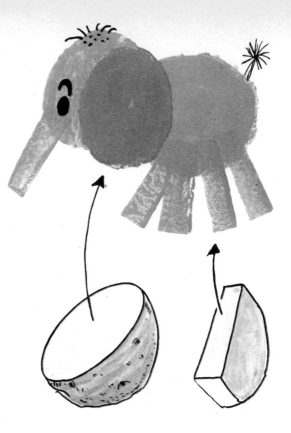

the paint will be easy to apply. Cut them up into the shapes you require for your picture and either put on the colour with a soft, broad brush or roll it on with a rubber roller like the one shown on page 10. When the potato "block"

is pressed against the paper the colour is trans-
ferred to the "thirsty" paper, which soaks up the
paint from the raw, moist potato. The elephant on

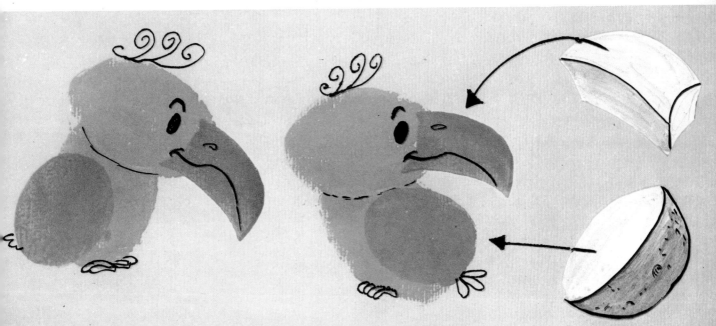

the left was printed with three different blocks. Hair, eyes and tail were drawn in afterwards. The decorated eggs were all printed in grey with the same block and the designs painted on afterwards. The pictures of the town and the funny birds were printed with blocks shaped as shown beside the pictures.

ARTIST'S EQUIP-MENT YOU CAN MAKE

The most important equipment for drawing and painting is, of course,

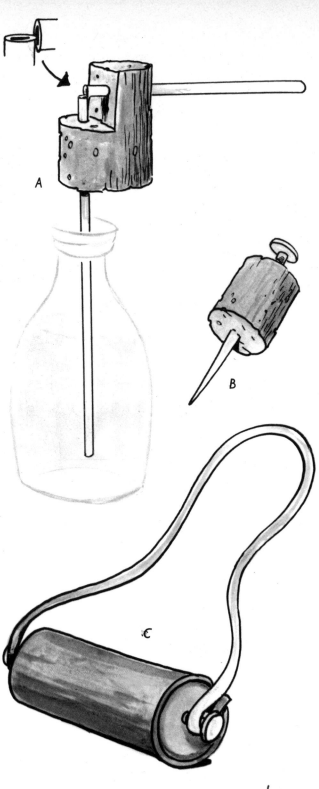

A Air spray
B Etching needle
C Roller
D Rubbing pad

A simple brush holder made from a large matchbox.

your pencils and brushes but in addition there are one or two other items you cannot do without: a) an air spray, b) an etching needle, c) a paint roller and d) a rubbing pad. All these can be bought in a shop but they are not difficult to make yourself.

Air spray: For this you need a cork from which you cut out a piece, and make two holes in it, as shown in the illustration. Through the holes you poke two tubes. The ends of the tubes must be placed against each other ex-

Two examples of brush holders which are easy to make.

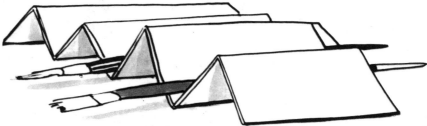

actly as shown in the small picture, otherwise the spray will not work. The spray is used to spray fixative over charcoal drawings which would otherwise be spoiled. It can also be used to apply paint, with or without stencils. (See example on page 30.) The liquid can be put in a jar or bottle.

The etching needle: consists of a nail which has been ground so that the point is smooth and sharp.

The paint Roller: consists of a piece of rubber

This beautiful butterfly is the result of a "folded" print.

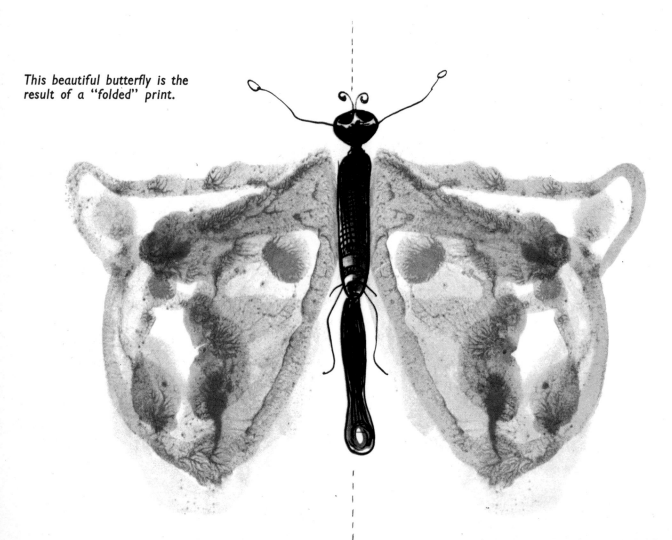

tube (garden hose) about 4 inches long. Through the tube you put a round piece of wood - a piece of broom handle, for instance - and fix a nail or screw in each end. The handle is made of strong steel wire, wound round the nails or screws.

The rubbing pad is made of a small piece of material, a ball of cotton wool and a rubber band. On page 40 is shown an example of how a rubbing pad is used.

BRUSH HOLDERS

You must look after your brus-

hes well and not let them lie around stiff with paint. On page 11 is shown some examples of some brush holders which are easy to make.

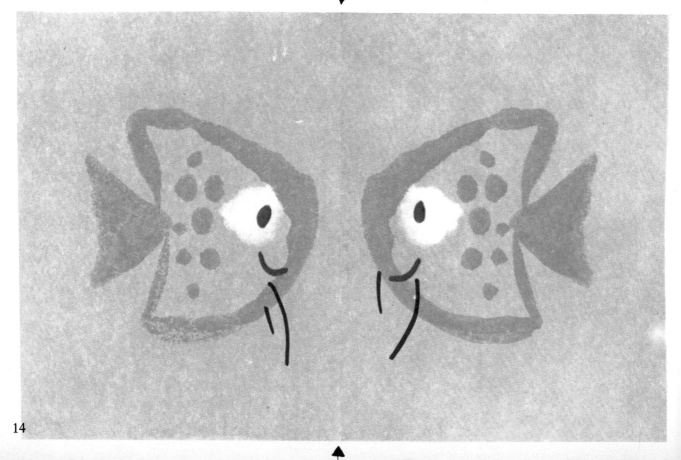

"FOLDED" PICTURES

The picture of a butterfly on page 12 is a "folded" picture, as are the pictures on page 14. The procedure is very simple. You daub a little paint on one half of a piece of paper, fold the sheet in the middle

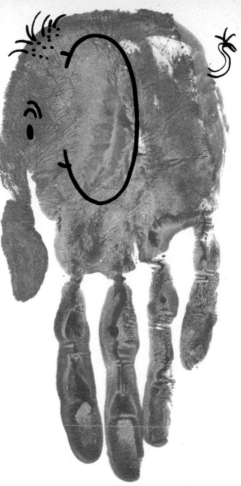

before the paint has dried and rub your hand lightly over the unpainted side of the paper. Open out the sheet again and let the paint-

15

ing dry. Then it is ready to be improved with a few strokes of the brush.

GENUINE HANDPRINTS

You can make an impression with practically everything. On page 15, for example, our artist has made hand prints which he completed with a few strokes of his pen. He simply smeared water colour on the palm of his hand and pressed it on the paper. It is worth noting that if a lot of hand prints are made in different colours on a large sheet of paper you can get some very amusing

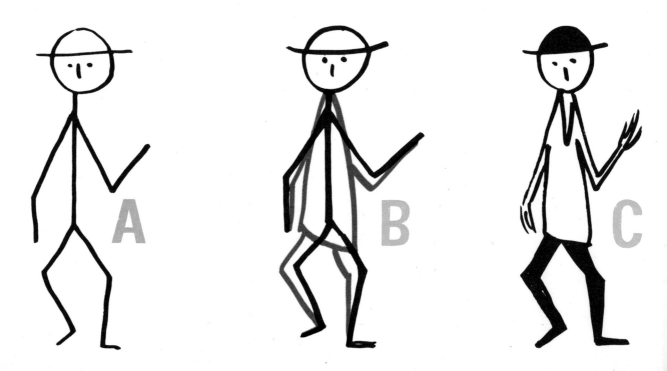

patterns. In this case, colour is the trick of the thing. You can also let the different colours go on to each other without spoiling the first print. These handprints look fine on paper covers for your school books but then you must, of course, lacquer the work with clear lacquer or fixative when the colours are dry.

HOW TO DRAW PEOPLE.

Anybody can draw a "pin" figure and it is a fact that everyone needs to know how to draw a more detailed figure. The pin figure A constitutes the "skeleton" and it is important that the different parts of the body are in the right proportions. Then you "dress" the figure with the help of extra strokes, B. Lastly rub out the skeleton and colour or ink in the drawing, C.

On page 17 are shown some examples of another method. You draw the outline of some simple figures with light strokes without lifting your pencil from the paper. Then ink in the figures, at the same time correcting any mistakes. Complete them with simple details of clothes. When you draw in this way you should not make the figures too detailed and finicky. The main thing is that they should look "alive." People drawn like this look fine in a picture of a town as shown in the chapter "Potato prints" on page 9.

With a stump of candle, a sheet of sandpaper and poster paints diluted with soap solution, you can make beautiful sandpaper lithographs. The result can be seen on the next page.

Sandpaper lithography.

This method of printing is best used for simple, uncomplicated motifs. The following material is used: a coarse sandpaper; a wax candle; paper and some kind of printers' ink. The ink can, for example, be black poster paint, blended with soap solution. First sketch out the motif with thin pencil strokes on the sandpaper, then fill in the outline with wax. You must press hard so that all the unevenness is filled in and the motif has a mirror-smooth surface.

Next, mix the printing ink with soap solution

A

so that it will stick to the greasy, wax surface, and roll it on to the sandpaper with a roller. When the ink is distri-

Figure A has been drawn on paper laid on a smooth surface ...

but figure B has been drawn on paper laid on a rough surface.

buted evenly over the wax, lay a piece of paper on it and rub your hand carefully on the back. The finished print looks just like a real lithograph!

B

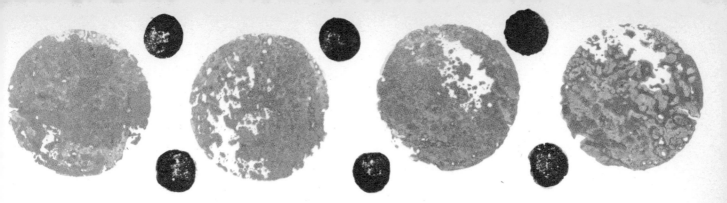

DRAWING WITH A ROUGH FOUNDATION

The old men A and B on the previous page look alike at first glance but figure A was drawn on paper which was laid on a smooth surface whereas figure B was drawn with the paper laid on a rough surface, in this case a coarse sandpaper. This method can be used in many cases; for example, if you want to draw bristles on a face, show coarse-textured material or draw a sandy beach. In the latter instance you should use a golden

Four leaf prints. See description on p. 23.

brown crayon. A file or anything with a rough surface can also be used as a foundation when you want to give a drawing a varied appearance.

CORK PRINTS

The border of oranges at the top of p. 21 was painted with poster paint smeared on a large and a small cork. It is really amazing how many beautiful prints you can make of simple, everyday objects. When you print with corks you can also use lacquer and because of this you can use the method even on hard surfaces such as glass, painted wood, etc.

These ten pieces of cardboard have been used as blocks in the printing of the Mexican on the next page.

LEAF PRINTS

Leaf prints such as those shown at the foot of p. 21 are easy to make. They can be very decorative and can be used in many ways. For example: on book covers, on personal picture post-cards, place cards, visiting cards or as a decoration on a piece of bea-utiful, plain stone which can be used as a paper-weight on your writing table. The procedure is easy. You simply brush a little water colour on the upper side of the leaf with a soft brush; lay the leaf, painted side down, on the paper and rub carefully with your finger. Lift the leaf off and the print is finished! You must be stingy with the paint so that you do not get any blots. The stalks are difficult to do without smearing the paper; it is

The picture above shows how, with a very simple motif, you can get an ordinary line drawing full of atmosphere and conjure forth depth without using shading.

▽ Henri Matisse

therefore neater to paint them in afterwards.

CARDBOARD PRINTS

The jolly Mexican was printed with the ten pieces of cardboard shown on p. 22. The red stripes on his sweater, his hair, eyes, nose and hat band were painted on afterwards. You can make very nice pictures and decorations by printing a whole row of men side by side. You can also vary the colours of their clothes just a little. Some men can have red sweaters and some can have blue trousers and so on. The same blocks can be used for all the men. To make it easy to handle the pieces of cardboard you should glue small pieces of paper on the backs. To these you

With a "double" pencil you can amuse yourself making abstract line drawings.

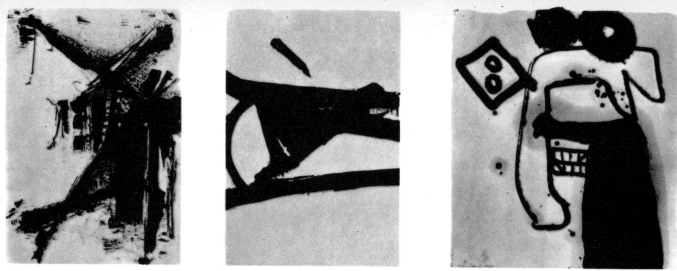

△ John Levee   △ Franz Kline   △ Allan Davie

can then fasten pins and with their help you can lift the blocks away after printing.

LINE DRAWINGS

With line drawing you usually make a picture using only strokes and lines and do not put in any work creating a contrast between the different spheres of a picture nor emphasize depth with the help of shading. When you look at the picture at the top of p. 24 you will see that even a simple line drawing can show atmosphere and give an impression of depth. In this picture the artist has achieved depth partly through the relative positions of the trees and partly because of the white moon in the back-ground. The picture is very uncomplicated - it has no horizon - but in spite of that it is full of atmosphere.

At the bottom of p. 24 and on this page are shown four more examples of line drawings done by four world-famous artists. From these pictures it is evident that an artist can even do abstract line drawings.

Top right is shown a three-colour melted wax print where the colours have been put one on top of another. Below are shown two single-colour prints.

On the left, a three-colour print where the colours have been put on simultaneously.

On p. 25 you will see an amusing example of how you can do an abstract line drawing.

MELTED WAX TECHNIQUE

The way you do this amusing method of printing is simple and cheap. You need a thin metal block or sheet, such as a tin lid, to use as a plate, and some wax crayons. First you warm the plate over a candle, radiator or gas ring but do not let it get too hot to handle without burning your fingers! Next you draw the motif on the plate with the wax crayons, then melt the colour and let it run a little. Lay a sheet of paper over it quickly and press it on the colour and the print is finished.

If you want to make a print in several colours you must print one colour at a time. In this case it is advisable to first draw the motif on the plate and at the same time make a mark on the edge of it and on the paper so that they may be easily matched up.

COPYING AND ENLARGING

With a little training you can soon learn to copy pictures by the simple method illustrated on p. 29. The only equipment you need is a ruler marked with inches, with the help of which you can copy, enlarge, reduce or even distort the original picture. First divide the illustration which is to be copied into squares, as shown, with each

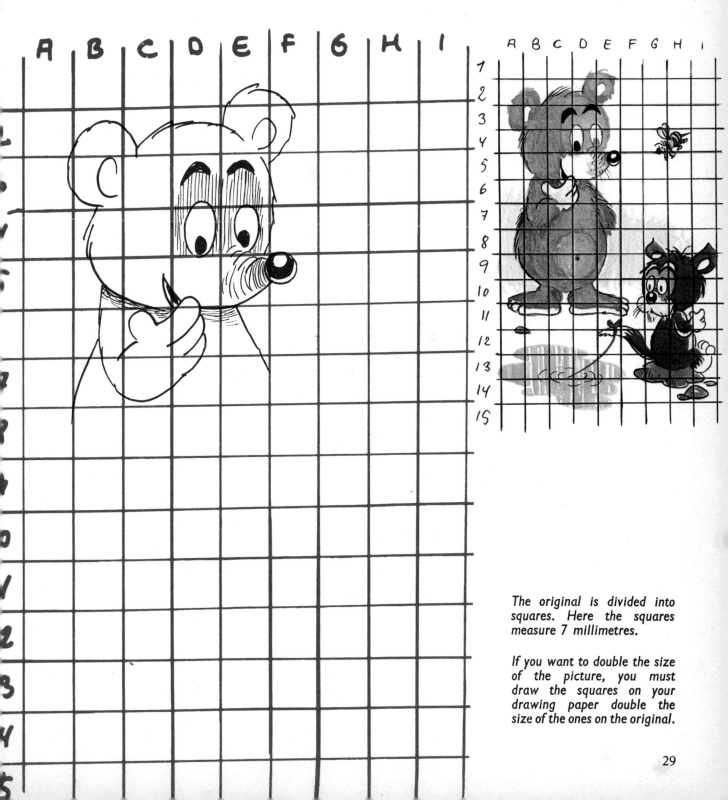

The original is divided into squares. Here the squares measure 7 millimetres.

If you want to double the size of the picture, you must draw the squares on your drawing paper double the size of the ones on the original.

Here you see the stencil which is used for spraying to make the bear on p. 31. Be careful to stand the right distance away for spraying. The nearer you hold the spray the bigger the dots will be. If you are not far enough away, the colour will run.

square, for example, half an inch square. The vertical rows are given letters and the horizontal ones numbers. On drawing paper you then rule up corresponding squares with faint pencil lines,

With a few simple brush strokes the picture is completed.

making the squares the same size as those on the original. If, however, you want your copy to be twice as large as the original, then you make the squares twice as large, and so on. To make the copy smaller all you have to do is make the squares proportionately smaller. If you want to distort the picture, rule up the original in rectangles but rule up your drawing paper in squares, just the same.

The motif is coloured by crayon, on top of which is brushed a layer of Indian ink diluted with soap solution.

When the ink is dry you scratch the picture with an etching needle.

SPRAY PAINTING

For this technique you use an air spray as de-

The short end of a
matchbox.

For the effects on this
page the following
scraping methods have
been used:

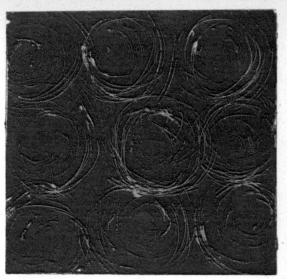

4 The small end of a
cork.

A broken matchstick

scribed on p. 10. On p.
30 you can see how to
use the spray and a sten-
cil. On p. 31 you can see
the result.

3 Scrunched-up paper

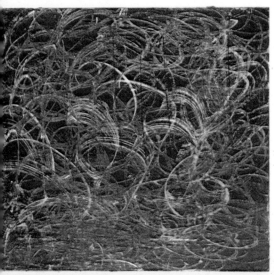

5 An ordinary comb.

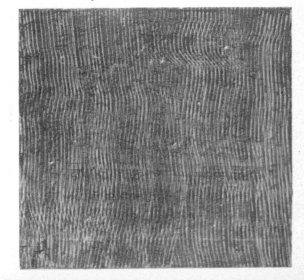

Fill the spray bottle with water and colour it with water colour. Next, cut a stencil which you lay over a sheet of paper and you are ready to start spraying. Be sure to get the right distance between the spray and the paper. It is important not to hold the spray too near or the colour will run. If you wish, you can spray several different colours on top of each other to get lovely bold pictures. Remember that each colour must dry before another is sprayed on!

SCRAPER METHOD

The motif is coloured with crayons, (wax or pastels). On top of the layer of colour you paint with Indian ink or water colour which has been blended with soap solution so as to stick on the greasy surface. When the colour is dry you carefully scrape the black layer with an etching needle so that the colour underneath

A rubber stamp mounted on a wooden block.

comes to the surface. If, instead of the etching needle, you use some of the objects mentioned on p. 33 you can easily make nice lid decorations for ornamental boxes and other things.

With a cut-off piece of rubber you can make decorative mosaics. (See p. 37 .)

LINO BLOCK PRINTING

Lino block printing is the most suitable method if you want to reproduce several prints from one block and do not require particular sharpness of outline and detail.

Blocks for this method can be made from many different materials. You can use rubber, leather and nylon or linoleum tiles. Of the last-named materials you can, with the help of special tools, make superior blocks which produce prints very like wood cuts.

If you make very small blocks they will be more easily handled if you stick them on to wooden blocks.

The printing procedure is the same as for

The procedure as described with plaster casts:
1 The runny plaster is put in a paper mould.
2 When the plaster has set, lift the sheet of glass away.
3 Engraving can begin.

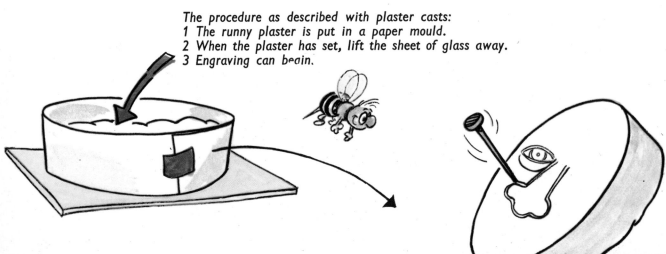

potato printing but the paint ought to be rather stiff. If the blocks are large they should be coloured with a roller.

MOSAIC PRINTS

The lower picture on p. 35 shows the method for making mosaic prints. You use only a stamp consisting of a narrow piece cut off a rubber. You can either sketch out the motif and then print the design, rubbing out the lines after-

wards, or, as in the example, draw the definite contours with Indian ink or water colours. The method is rather time consuming and for this reason it is essential, in order to avoid mistakes, that you make

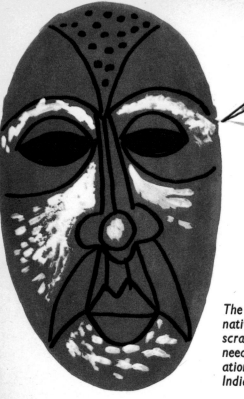

The white parts of the native mask have been scraped with an etching needle. The black decoration is painted on with Indian ink. (See p. 39.)

an accurate colour sketch before the printing is be-gun.

PLASTER PRINTS

Plaster printing is a rather more advanced method of printing. The procedure is somewhat like that of wood-engraving but the material is more easily worked. The prints which you can produce with plaster blocks look rather like wood cuts. Compare both pictures on p.37. The top one is a wood cut by the German artist Emil Nolde while the picture in blue at the bottom is a plaster print.

The block itself is cast in plaster. The runny plaster is poured into a paper mould which is placed on a sheet of glass. When the plaster sets and is dry right through, the cast is lifted away from the glass and the mould taken off and you will have a plaster cast with an even and smooth bottom surface. On this surface you then engrave the motif with an etching needle. Large white parts can be hollowed out with a chisel or knife but with a light hand so that no cracks are made in the plaster. When the motif is engraved, roll printers' ink over it with a roller and you can begin printing.

CARDBOARD GRAFFITO

Here the etching needle returns to use. This time you use it as a substitute for white opaque. The method is like the scraper method shown on p. 3 , but

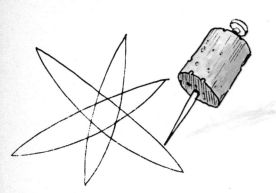

here you work only with a layer of colour. You can paint with Indian ink or water colour but you can also use quick-drying lacquer. With the latter you can also work on art board with a glossy surface. When the colour has dried you sketch out the motif with faint pencil lines. The motif

should not be too detailed as the work ought to be done on a rather large surface to make the scraping easier. Scrape away the colour in the parts and lines which you want to be white so that the surface of the board emerges.

The mask up on the left on p.38 is made on the same principle as the picture down the bottom of p.39 but for the mask red has been used with black lines.

RUBBINGS

Here the rubbing pad comes into use. The star at the top of p.40 was made in the following way: A star was carved on a piece of soft cardboard with the help of an etching needle. Carved so hard that the lines went right through to the back of the cardboard. Then the board was laid with the back upwards, a sheet of drawing paper placed over it and rubbed with the rubbing pad which had first been spread with colouring matter, which had been ground in from the point of a coloured pencil.

The example at the foot of p.40 was made in another way. For this a figure was cut out of cardboard and the pieces glued on a sheet of paper. Drawing paper was laid on it and the work then proceeded exactly as in the previous example.

CONTOUR DRAWING

To work with abnormally thick lines can sometimes be very effective. The motif itself ought naturally to be adapted to the method and consequently rather simple and uncomplicated in colour and form. But you can also use thick lines in drawings which you are not very pleased with and you will greatly improve them. The result is that all fields of colour are given a lift and become more brilliant even if the colours themselves are dull. The picture on the opposite page illustrates this clearly. If the artist had used ordinary lines the colours used would have appeared pale and uninteresting.

PERSPECTIVE

It is often rather difficult to get the right perspective and proportions when drawing an object obliquely from in front. In such a case you can use a method we will call "stacking boxes." You imagine you are putting the object into boxes whose sides exactly enclose the object you are drawing. By the very fact that you can then work with straight parallel

lines it becomes easier to get the right perspective and proportions. All the vertical lines must be parallel and all the horizontal lines should start at an angle to each other.

You begin by determining the outer measure of the object and divide the drawing into different "boxes" whose number and relative proportion is determined by the appearance and form of the object. (The rough lines in red in the example.) Naturally you must make the lines as faint as possible so that they can be rubbed out afterwards. You can then draw proper lines in the "boxes," draw in with Indian ink and rub out the "boxes."

SPOILT DRAWINGS

Now and then you are bound to let your pen or brush slip and the result will be an annoying blot. But a little imagination and a few simple strokes will transform the ugly blots into amusing figures.

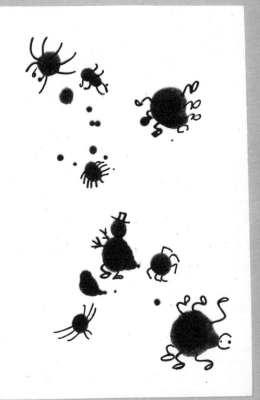

In the same series:

CUTTING, FOLDING AND GLUEING

a book of how-to-make

silhouette pictures

mosaic cut-outs

mobiles

masks

matchstick pictures

etc.

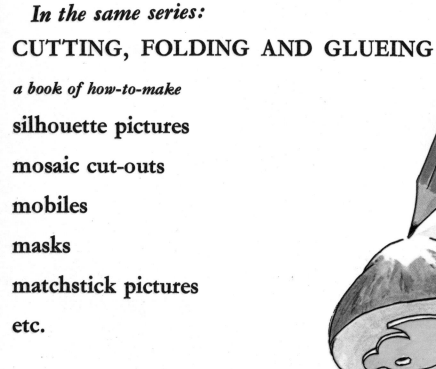